DENISE RILEY is a critically acclaimed writer of both philosophy and poetry. She is Professor Emerita of the History of Ideas and of Poetry at UEA. Her visiting positions have included A.D. White Professor at Cornell University in the US, Writer in Residence at the Tate Gallery in London, and Visiting Fellow at Birkbeck College in the University of London. She has taught philosophy, social history, art history, and writing. Denise Riley lives in London.

LUREX

Denise Riley

PICADOR

First published 2022 by Picador
an imprint of Pan Macmillan
6 Briset Street, London EC1M 5NR
EU representative: Macmillan Publishers Ireland Limited, 1st Floor,
The Liffey Trust Centre, 117–126 Sheriff Street Upper, Dublin 1 DO1 YC43
Associated companies throughout the world
www.panmacmillan.com

ISBN 978-1-5290-7813-8

1 3 5 7 9 8 6 4 2

A CIP catalogue record for this book is available from the British Library.

Printed and bound by CPI Group (UK) Ltd, Croydon, CR0 4YY

Visit **www.picador.com** to read more about all our books
and to buy them. You will also find features, author interviews and
news of any author events, and you can sign up for e-newsletters
so that you're always first to hear about our new releases.

To Albertine and Mira

Contents

LUREX

'Please supply a biographical note'

A natal error.
Steadied by pamphlets
and brilliance of the babies.
In leaping joy alone.
Why do some will themselves to stone.
Now is it time for night to fall.

What the lyric said

I'd thought a song
went like this. I should
have known.

The neighbours are kind
also loud, out
in the hot gardens.

How could I
have known. *Fuck,*
fuck, they warble.

Committed

You're born with dead children in your body.
Some reach daylight, others won't – although

even the walkers in sunshine go streaming to
those short homes you hollowed out for them –

nippy from infancy, they'll dart ahead of you
narrowing, tinier, into their vanishing points.

Whether they'd come to love its fleshiness or
not, you did force life on dear future corpses.

You, a sexton dug in between two worlds, or
you, a metronome, tracking their fluent feet –

all of you in the dark as to what you'd started.
They forgive you by (with luck) outliving you.

Not Olga

A canvas bawled scarlet —
one eye heard it. Flesh
a grey-mauve coil, clean
on its yellow chair. Skin
tinged violet, pea green.
Exquisite slug! Best done
in oils, not circumscribed.

Seaside rock

No novelties but the very same tenacious lettering running all the way through like a stick of seaside rock that stays readable wherever along its length it gets snapped. Those letters might declare 'Brighton' or 'Blackpool' or 'Margate'; even crunched nearly their whole way down, they'd still keep legible. They could equally well say 'Elizabeth', since they'd read as faithfully whatever way they're broken. 'You can't turn some old-school, two-bit, Brit candy into a metaphor for her?' Yes but only in lettered constancy. Properly fierce, while generous, such stalwart style, if cut, shows comic flair − it always runs right through.

I get through

One drawback of loneliness: you can notice yourself too much, carrying this self around between cupped hands like something fragile in need of careful positioning, although you'd not meant to become a thing to yourself, far less a delicate fetish. Yet once you've ferried your own cloistered burden outdoors, any breeze will undo it, so by then you're no longer a well-wrapped patted ball, but are genially uncoiled on the air, dispersed as filaments apt to take a wandering interest in everything, bar their source. Both working and living alone, I might wait days for a sighting of anyone familiar; still, hours may slip by with reassuring ease if my violin's sobbing can swing to a chirped pizzicato. Bookish daffs aside, a bright solitude beams gaiety upon my inward eye but it can lurch to self-upbraiding: what eager emptiness made me incapable of holding onto someone else's affections? Don't rush to answer. My DIY tussles allow me an alibi: being of use. So what if my plastering's done in place of some living contact. Faced by the freshly polished table, set for one, I'll quaver that 'we're born alone, we die alone'. But am not heartened by this saw. Too laboured, these efforts to handle seclusion gracefully. But then, it'd be harder to *not* be alone – or at least, so I fancy, rehashing this half-convinced solace – 'I wouldn't much like to be *visible* to someone else all the time; not that I do anything so wicked in private – sadly'. Being solo means calculating; might I tot up enough friends to see each one per week, over the year but how many of those might come round more (or less) often? What a rainbow of Post-It Notes a hope-stuffed timetable needs. Why was humanity fabricated as pinpricks of single perception?

Sequestered minds, embodied – a theatrically bad arrangement. Simpler, kinder, for just one collective to have been engineered un-individuated – rather than us billions of scrapping creatures. The plain truth is that, given the longed-for company, I'll love it but soon get overwhelmed, then want to slip off home – and do, to the joy of flopping alone with a drink that's riskily comforting. Unseen (yes, glad of that) I'll uncurl for an evening's preparing; death-sorting through my clothes in heaps, lamenting garments where grubs of moths revolved my cashmere pensively between their jaws, am a cloth snake of a draft-excluder wedged in gaps, my one side warmed, the other chilly (is it late enough now for this twilight's single malt?) Cheered as I cheaply am by a small small plant's lumpy name – an ageratum, its button-like washy mauves set on my worktop where rough-ribbed sunflowers lour across it – no, nothing turns 'gratefully' to catch the sun. – Yet turn it will. I'll lay me down. Today has just been got through.

From René Char's vineyard

Evening rosary of grapes.
The highest bunch bleeds a last glitter.
Brother larch, moss spur, quick harp.
Were a swift to land, it'd rip open.
Friends of picnicking in hailstorms, don't die off yet.
Got a light, got the time, how far's the next town?
Pine trunks tighten into beds into hexagons.

Lines from 'Novalis'

Language is Delphi.
A house is a complex box.
Children are antiquities
yet not all children are children.

The *acoustic* nature of the soul.
Nature gradually secretes us again;
perhaps it is a reciprocal secretion.
All misery repels the weak.

Something critical is everywhere.
The moralised breast. Water
is a wet flame. The greatest works
of art afford us no *pleasure* at all.

Obsession with 'originality' is coarse.
Every Englishman is an island.
Why ever do we need a beginning?
Few human beings are human beings.

And home lamenting bore it

Hose down the bloody lamb.
Shear its woolly skin to the bone.
Penitential rain, cleanse my remembering.
Mop me in blue scrubs.
Mother of mercy, when we were thin!

Prize Cultures

He is battling another highly-regarded poet for the prestigious annual *Northern Vaunter*.

Her work is hotly tipped for an award for *Flagrant Though Delicate Self-Promotion*.

She is expected to carry off the *Triple Smash Of Humblebraggers* effortlessly yet modestly.

Her Under-18 prize includes mentoring by that radical poet who won a coveted *Silkiest Text*.

'They' is storming the Recommendeds for *International Pronouns Of Boldness* (mine was always 'it').

He took first place for 'most innovative mullet' in the *Great Lyric Hair* contest of 1979.

He's since been shortlisted five times for a global *Grudgingly Respected If Privately Disliked*.

Their collaborations for the new *Experimental Malevolence* prize really wowed the judges.

They've now withdrawn from the ethically-sensitive PoundLand Residencies.

She beat off strong competition in the *Deeply Sad But Beautifuls* which we are all so excited about.

It's just destroyed its hopes of also-ran in the *Kindly Pensioner Poets* stakes — not an expanding field.

1948

i

Your past can't tell it *is* the past.
How to convince it that it's done with, now?
The only touches that I got before I reached eighteen were blows.
It never crossed my mind to look for others' kindness, later on.
Though my pigheaded will alone propelled me to my sorrows.

ii

When I could step into the shockingly open world
I wasn't sure of where I ended, or where someone else began.
This was a joyous state.
Under my skin I might have been a man, a kindly one.
Longing leaped in flames, it raced and crackled.
Small winds tore through it, keening
and fanning its chase.
It made the truest of songs –
it was the truth ablaze,
it was pure wanting, bloodied and radiant.
Holy, holy, sang that pursuit
and holier the infants born of it.
Then unholy the contempt that circled me.

iii

Time did, but did not, pass
in muted work and stabs of gaiety
to build some way for us to live
clear of the glaring yet repeated risks
of coupledom warped by rancour.
A darling can turn wolfish.

iv

I wished, half-helpfully, to be unseen
or run a website for the hard-to-place
with me as its founder member.
Now I'll brandish my rosy face around
flaunting my pratfalls of a baffled need
while hope deferred still hollows me out,
takes clownish leaps about my gouged-out shell.

v

As there's dark humour in a darker time
so there's resilience in an obvious rhyme.

Self-parody deflates a plaintive mime
to make it truer – just *as* pantomime.

vi

The mothers are long dead,
the several fathers too.
What took place is done, though
it murmurs on in you
who got through it alive, with
a bit more extracting to do.

vii

On blackened streets the taint was scoured from doorsteps.
The illegitimate sent off to the infertile,
their pasts expunged, their names altered.
Their records sealed.
No need to mention any of it again.
That was only for the best, it was all for the best.
Everyone meant it for the best.

viii

This present-past hangs on. It says:
'Days flocked with frighteners — they'll circle round you still
though they're long dead who daily clouted you across the mouth —
disgusting animal, you're asking for it, useless object, you want a good thrashing.
You didn't, but you got it anyway, with other things far better not
to get (though, decades later, getting pregnant saved your life
since you did get lovable children). Slaps smelled of bleach
striping your face in wheals each the width of the finger
that made them — you prayed that they'd fade before school.
A knee to the small of your back shoved you down
if you paused on the stairs: *you're bad — bad, through and through.*
You spend your next sixty-eight years working out how far that's true.
So what are you asking for now? To not still hear
these utterances, in the only mother-tongue you knew:
obey without question, you want a real beating, spare the rod
spoil the child, shut your gob or I'll shut it for you
you're neither use nor ornament, you're not like other girls
you don't deserve to be loved, you belong in the loony bin
a child has to have its spirit broken, hold your tongue
you disobedient animal, no one would ever believe you
— Well, no. Though you'd never expected them to.
Who would have heard you then, who would,
since no one could see how you'd tried to be good.
You can't try any harder than ever you could.'

ix

'That couldn't have happened, you seem so normal.'
– I am so normal. And it did.
Just as it did to thousands.

x

I tell my past it's passed, though it can't tell.
More training, to teach obedience: the toddler
who'd wet herself gripped by the scruff of her neck
and her nose rubbed in it, in freshly damp white cotton.
Their real beloved dog I envied, while I stayed an 'it'
burrowing through straw quills in the kennel
to study the grace of the dog, to poach the secret of being liked.
Yet gradually my life as an 'it' has grown muscular.
Almost, I am that dog.

xi

I won't blame those enslaved by their own rages,
fearful of a baby that would never feel like theirs
but couldn't be returned to the agency.
I blame the powers that packed us off to them
as misconceived children to be conformed –
easy mishaps in small border towns,
slurs on their working families.

xii

Cast to the winds, some might find safe landings,
yet others blew onto steel shards.
'Bad blood' was how our bad fortunes described us.
It could all have worked out fine – bar the tick
of a chancy official biro, handing you straight
to the care of gloved anger, or respectable angry anxiety.
But that was the luck of it, that was how it fell out
for surplus postwar children.
The indifferently falling rains of them.

xiii

'More care would get taken in re-homing a dog.'
Though the dog might at least have its pedigree.

Hit and miss (literally) where you ended up.
And each person involved was unknowing.

xiv

This history's too commonplace to tell.
It is a story which so many own.
How do I get it right, alone?
The point of telling is to crack its spell.

xv

'The point of telling is to crack its spell'?
What if it underscores dead violence
as calligraphy – a sentence
maybe freeing, but only if 'done well'?
And when the casual judgements fly
around each teller: 'She's damaged. TMI'?
– Judgement runs everywhere in our material.

'Friend and reader of Horace'
(after Günter Eich)

Don't keep going on about Horace
and 'learning to die'.
No one learnt that,
it just happened to them
like being born.

A thing in a room

Wooden ladder smeared in

dried paint, spatters & drifts

of it, old speckles sunk deep

in the grain, daubed, flecked

as I'm braced, sleek brush to

hand, at wilful ease – though

on some lower rung – heavy

struts clop hard to, as I lug it

round the emulsioned walls'

high cloudy layers; ingrained

pasts, scarred-cream hazards.

White spirit! scrub the painter

clear of the wood – clean off.

'Beggars of Life'

The movie is over, yet the screening reels on through your eyes – you've left the cinema, but you're still seeing 'in' graceful Ozu, or 'in' kindly Kore-Eda, or in pleats, in blood, or plain rose; you're passing by nondescript shopfronts now floodlit in scarlet, thanks purely to Coutard's lens, or another occasion's pearly sorrow has slicked down these pavements, where men lope in torrents of rain that could flatten that one bar they want – it must be a plywood prop. In the dark you'd been watching a storm that will not die down in the light. So how come a film's world-outlook keeps radiating from your own eyeballs – not its set, least of all its ideas – but its whole 'feel', its tinge or angles? Louise flicked her bob until it refashioned your mop to shine by the end of 'Beggars of Life' – as in Burnett's 'Killer of Sheep', an 'of' in the title holds promise – you too are 'of' your last-viewed movie, generously unspooling outside itself while subtitles flash up unasked, like Farhadi's captions on judgment: 'Each side wants to understand the other but their situation compels them to fight'. You wish. Heels pivot, or are clicked, in the elongated spans between people. Your feet were slipped into others' seamed nylons, then eased into kid shoes. It was me-too in 'La Notte' and that dawn grew milky-sour. Maybe Martel's lucid camera has cornered you – shut tight in her car, its rolled up windows bouncing the sunlight so inward you'd scarcely see out, bar a blurry column of what might be human figures. 'Grief' is too bland a word, and I've always found it irritating, all the more so since he died, but I couldn't really say why;

although, movie-loving spectator, I can read *your* diagnosis of why, embossed in bold on your face. Return to us, you subtler Jeanne Moreau, ripe doubter; sulk hotly on the 19 bus nudging its way through a right smog of implication. Step forth, doe-eyed Monica, let your wide freckled cheekbones gleam again out of your shadows. But that beauty's long sunk in her aching monochrome. Brilliantine'd heads are still hauling the length of canals of string vests – while no probation officer will lecture you again: 'a working class man would have battered you, you should be thankful he's only trying to remove the children.' We'll have no more 'in love' though the moon be, &c. The incensed air looms rich with pondering saxes – to be 'confessional' must mean there's something *to* confess, but what is that thing's true name? Nico, chanteuse remixed velvety, remarked 'I wasn't happy when I was beautiful'. It's you who are in the wrong, you who were both born in it and born into it. But that's wrong, too. Hell-bent on thinking the best of others, who might yet turn out to be kind, you wouldn't 'draw the consequences' – wanting no consequences but reliable love. Twilight sags blue on the terrace, the clinks of the party dim as long-lashed looks pan out across olive groves branched like squirrel-hair brushes, handy enough for rouge; neither 'the male' nor the female gaze, but the gaze of the movie itself, suffusing your vision until it wears off, after loaning its clips of ten divine-enough minutes. Then back my duller daily outlook comes. I'll fight against letting it blanket me in its colourised rereleases of the out-of-the-blue cruelty of someone I'd trusted – I've sat through that movie before, too often; have lain on its cutting-room floor. Still – here is Resnais, or filmic joy. It is good to be old, though it's perilous.

[23]

To a Lady, viewed by a Head-Louse

I with my triumphant bites
Vex useless human parasites.
You world-devourers are for – what?
'Useful' you yourselves are not.
Refer me, lady, to your Gaia –
My jaws will raise your blush of fire.
When humans pause to think of me
It makes their skin crawl eerily;
Parasitosis – their deluded
Dread that ghost nits have intruded.
It's my sole work to multiply –
The task of ladies to ask 'Why
Should such a pointless breed exist?'
Only the entomologist
Admits my 'good-for-nothing' species
To own the interest of its faeces
For those can raise allergic wheals
Then mortified parental squeals
Or groans of mums or dads who find
Their darlings' hair home to my kind,
Each louse egg's tight-cemented pearl
Superglued to their shampooed girl.
I'll plant rosettes of telltale red
High on her neck, low on her head
Until your steel rake catches me
Or unguents loose their fatal sea.
Fleas acquire some charming tropes

For amorous fluid-mingling hopes –
Lice? Condemned to Owen's trench
By reportage of mud-blood stench.
Some sorts make meals for grooming birds
While others have engendered words
Like 'lousy', apt for human speech –
Each *head-louse* purely is for each.
My species' world obeys no brief
Of reciprocity – such a relief
Not to claim virtue. Ah, your 'rich
Biodiversity'! Makes you itch.
I am for nothing – only to increase
My number, after my decease.
'Purposeless' insects may prove good
For squashing pieties that we should
Match human myths of mutual aid –
Vain fantasy we lice downgrade.
Lady, I'd answer Robbie Burns:
Let other species take their turns
And do not keep so dour and mean
Vaunting your old Anthropocene.

Plaguey winter

Long welt of sneaking dawn, pleated
to a cold glow on still-black curtains.

Some tinny bird, scraping out there
at its night: zeal, puffed up for rivals.

*

Your eyes, shut or open, get crowded
in coloured pinpricks surging around

on the slatey air of your bedroom –
you, a membrane between two darks.

*

Please let an early underground train
nudge & trundle down punctual tracks

whose lines loop far below this house –
then you'd overhear people unfurling.

*

A sky like putty, hours before daybreak,
yawns as it waits and then turns grainy

settling to orangey grey. The rest
you'll manage. Again, you'll fill today.

Is there nobody in here?

A bay ground out between high rocks, skirting of dark cliffs, rocky foothills, blunt outcrops fringed on their lower slopes with ruffs of alder and birch. Thin path by the flurried burn, foam snagged on cress, a strayed montbretia's orange flecks. Oaks shaved by the wind like flat-topped thorns. Wide plain a wash of grasses. Abandoned hay meadows turned to sedge, fields blurred, edgeless, yellowing; moleskin bulrushes lashed over their own pools of rustling. Reed-beds stream in pinkish plumes, flossy on hollow stalks, sharp-angled leaves flapping. Grazed salt marshes, lapped by scatterings of small boulders, tar-streaked and laced with dried bladder-wrack, blown into rough crescents coiling their trails of silvery sand, blackened. Waterfall: a pillar against far cliffs, a standing cream column.

Another Agony in the Garden

The harshness in a human face adores its closeness to the bone.
It glories in refusing to yield. It patrols its own numbed attitude
sealed off from another's despair, to guard its air of being strong.

A fox that strolls in broad daylight has something shameful to disown:
a half-buried relic he's scraped up, worried at, gingerly chewed,
his hours of seclusion to gnaw it clean compelled to be overlong.

A child who knows its love repulsed steadies to bed itself in stone
then will get even more despised for lacking in proper gratitude.
Convinced it is to blame for not being kindly ushered in among

the good, its feeling's wordless – more of a subdued animal moan
at a gleam of slim aquamarine rivulets snaking by a painted wood;
the good's snap verdict ('must move on') is inexperienced and wrong.

An ear that's cocked in sympathy with the rock-bound solitary's groan
and attuned to His rasping egrets, twin comics of divine fortitude,
still hears its own self as isolated – so guaranteeing it can't belong.

'You knew how to pick 'em, all right', tease the friends who aren't alone.
I never 'picked' anyone – felt lucky to get auditioned, or even viewed.
Am I, thanks to that feeling, a source of a darkness my best efforts prolong.

The moth that trembles in the night blunders around to find her clone.
Her tiny shuddering engagements will chafe away to powdery solitude.
Discarded persons pummel their exasperating 'shame/blame' singsong.

Be quick

I've no companion
bar a shadow
pointing backwards.

Dear life, don't ghost me yet!
Find me a home
through stumbling rain.

None of it adds up

Painstakingly dug, those narrows. Luminous a slit of sky above.
Warm onrushes of conviction, later denied. So. All gouged out.

I could grasp their leaving, but not the mutilating that followed.
Hadn't I been killed off trimly enough to seal my worthlessness?

But there they were right. To be worthless: a glory. Not counting,
I swan with the chatty dead – numberless uncalculating familiars.

How does anyone get over these things

A light thought of dog roses, with pale honeysuckle
slopping over the lane, furred clematis buds arched
from streaked wood, arrowy leaves serried to point
the walker's way coiled round in bindweed wreaths
to crown her that glowing Rhine's 'distant beloved'
as she, composed if mildly mutinous, sinks beneath
its waters. At least no man in his car will ever again
instruct her: 'You can say goodbye to the children –
I've planned this "accident" so you will die, not me
nor them, just you – I'm driving straight across this
oncoming lane.' Can I subdue a lurid, sadly factual
past that keeps searing me through with my blame?
Might I be less bumbling in my back-flips from 'she'
to 'I', done in a belief that 'I' is often transpersonal?
Could I turn nonchalant, cool as a peremptory gaze
from some noble COS model online? But wistfulness
is a sweetener to bloom in shade; is pure belladonna.
So was it *circa* 1799 when she was a damp 'beloved'?
Dusk packed it in, long since. The old shames rouge
a thinly-buffered skin, below which there is yowling.

'What are you working on?'

Someone will ask me
'What are you working on?'
On nothing, I'll say. To be
worked *on* – that'd be luck –

such 'being worked on'
could throw out a rare spark
from the language-engine's
indifferent grinding.

Its own reverbs tune
some dispassionate jabber
tweezing white noise from
a skull's ric-rac sutures.

Or am I tone-deaf to
old radio frequencies
in the glare of this stillness
that waits, incurious –

but no lament's needed
should a human receiver
fail to bear that light
clatter where no ear is.

Any driven animal

Anonymous animal of the yellow hide,
scat – go figure out the curio of why
your louring passions stump about for more,
lowing that they'd get filleted per usual,
their dewlaps swaying to some charmer's wind
then eyeballed by the taxidermist. Lighter
to wear a dress of feathers and eat berries,
slice dapper arcs of wingtip self-sufficing,
spiral above the leaves, rattle the heather.
But no, your portly body's earthed, perplexed –
tramples at night to know itself unsexed.

Three awkward ears

i

It rains it rains shepherdess, rains on the river — as
if on thicker liquids, cream or latex, raindrops stot it
to pitted rings in water, which swell to hoops of water.

Up gallop young men, each of them pleasingly sharpened
to hunt down dormant crepitus in smooth sprawled limbs
since, speaking botanically, flowering's a sign of distress.

Beribboned looms the large one, stolid in his pastel satins
who was ever gravely loving but was not much loved back —
he's ruffed for the arching gleam and flop of tulip heads.

Some buxom clouds lollop along, gloweringly under-lit
past russet trees brushed dark, fine-feathered by sable hair.
What's that inhuman call, far into the woods of no ears.

ii

High confident calling
to no one it knows of
from no throaty talker
nor squirreled in ears
it fans out to soar over
gaping-jawed screens
or dilate that one iris as
purplish as hearts whose
it isn't – so, pulsating to
mouth every anyone, it
uncoils as invoking –
opens its confiding peal.

iii

ice-burned tongues
clump into celestine's
eye-blue spar & chink
on snow-muffled ears

Facts of the 1950s

Within seven days, God (so you were instructed at school) had created the world so perfectly that He'd even embedded fossils in rocks, in order to trick and expose anyone who espoused the heresy of evolution. In the kitchen at home, iron pails held sheep's heads being steeped to make Scotch broth, a few long yellow teeth loose in their liquid. Other pails of cold water came and went every few weeks. Those were to soak the white cloths, seeping out their clouds of blood. Saint Theresa, who should by rights be painted wreathed in rose petals, always wore her cocoa-brown veil. In a spirit of huge calm, you understood perfectly that you were bound for a prison where you'd be locked up in solitary for life. You'd need to occupy yourself throughout this coming sentence, so you invented and rehearsed many silent word games. Though what if you ever ran out of them?

Person on train in August

I was alive, but I paid for it heavily. Oh fair
enough, although my coin was sex-specific.
I cupped such tenderness in both hands
and nowhere could accept it. Now, easing by
this railway cutting, rife with buddleia snouts
— bull terriers' profiles solemn white, crinkled
in mauve, or rusting brown at cocky angles —
we will shortly be arriving at Tale Parochial
where our journey ends [. . .] *all our belongings.*

Unlike

Appalled, yet flexy as a marionette
remoulded far from children and from men
it tries itself before its own star chamber –
recoils in stammers. Cannot answer, she.
In mounds of rainy violets, no aid hides;
court of itself-condemned admits no plea
of how she tried so hard or what the petals saw
from their quite harmless rosette of leaves.

(i.m. Tom Raworth)

'Songs Without Words'

It's odd to recall
'sweet the mouth in its quiet'
yet keep an ear open
for what's gone a-fowling

that cawed for its tea
singing Felix's motto
down the long day's stream
& away over the burnet

(i.m. John James)

Tick tock

A formal structure generates your thought.
Your mind will follow where the meter leads.
A poet hardly merits that 'well-wrought'
tick of approval from her critic, if he reads

her work for 'crafting' as its afterthought
of content; as if her lighter artifice needs
to trap in prosody what she'd first fought
to formulate in prose; as if her text proceeds

to turn 'poetic' a philosophy. Her retort:
that rhythm's own dictation soon exceeds
prior deliberation – cadence will thwart
prosaic forethought, as its ear lip-reads –

so 'sense must seem an echo to the sound'.
A natural music makes this turnaround.

Burying the brittle book of abandonment

You sodden pages, flop over the black waves
to bring back, bring back that cold one to me

whose implacable tale's turned rigid, to block
its own sorrow; ossifies your hand-sewn spine.

Book of salt tears, be beached to lie encrusted
with mottled ivory limbs of hollowed crabs —

your grave burrowed out under sands inching
around horned poppies, crumpled rock-roses

on dunes gripped hard by marram, narrowed
to seal your binding — as stilled your sounding.

At 'Plumage House'

A smothering downy air – of ibis, marabou,
of scalloped bustard, also the shaggy rhea,
of grebe, egret, emu, a condor's shiny quills
the lollipop toucan, colouring-book macaw,
& ostrich plumes. Kittiwake, clean-cut tern
cheaper, unglamorous, serviceable on hats.
Halved lyre-birds, gutted, dried to torques.
Baled wings from lustrous birds of paradise
in 'millinery ready' carmine, jet or emerald.
Or modish sapphire? *'Ladies, ladies.'* – *'Men!'*

'All, as a rule, fall towards their wound'

Sheathed in their amber, dove grey, olive silk
saints clutch a grill or wheel, pincers or spear;
calm heads anointed by the buttery sunlight
incline to these instruments of their torture
turned to starred, yet unvarnished, blazons
as cloaks drip carmine and rose velvets glow.
Here the raised axe is no more than its action:
it hands the decapitated to their merciful rest.
Would it help me a bit to stroke its mild blade,
take the edge off old violence; though not gild
it later, by announcing 'Blessedly, I survived'.
What hope is there of a purely secular grace?
Attend, Agnes; your white emblem's bleating.

Lurex

Hush, jeremiads, flat as milk
where not bubbling under the blood.
And I myself in cramoisie.

The fathers look to their veins.
The blood has it. Could they not have
trusted in themselves, and so in us.

Not easy in their leaving:
'How do I know it's mine?'
How am I mine, who once was yours.

Dark yet sparkly —
the seriousness of it!
To believe in both its *then* and its *now*.

A child as a guarantor
against loneliness, including its own:
one fact that is kinder all round.

From 'Alice, a fragment'

Young men were 'poets', in their velvet loons. Reclining on that title, they'd press upon you copies of their poems or latest pamphlets: bower birds, with self-reflecting gifts churned out on duplicators. But nesting instincts smartly swung to angry pecks, then flitting off; from lofty habitats shearwaters' vanguard wings sliced over the river with its shored-up banks, miscalled 'the mainstream' down which a very few could merrily row their boat when life was but a dream – the dream of revolution.

I didn't want 'a voice' myself, far less that 'woman's voice' . . . My feminism fled such retro-femininity, as it then appeared. Not womanly, my shameless hopes. So prices were to pay, as usual – yet these weren't on display. I scraped the lining of my skinny purse through harsher miseries than carping verse; but St Mark's seraphim rose to blaze, with Alice fearless among them, surefooted in the luminous confiding of her calling.

'And as I sit I feel the gaze'

Eyes brush across your face – you sense their touch settle
as if a fly had lit upon your cheekbone for its promenade,
while some eyes you feel more as a bold tap at your skin:
'What's up in there?' Soon bored, they flick off smartish.
Optics must have it wrong; the eyeballs surely do extrude
their rays like feelers, whisking round their object, as any
glanced-at face, even a back, intuits. Hopeless to caution
the scanning eye 'Keep off me' – an unfocused look *just is*
promiscuous, however it swivels, zooms dazedly, or plain
falls where it may, as casually as snow, and as blanketing.
Still, sheared of the coating of a gazer's squint, you're left
naked on the heath with a myriad of the blessedly unseen
whose skins aren't glazed by a latex of stares. That other
may, the hawthorn, whose urine-scented creaminess lolls
heaped as if a big flour-sifter had been tipped up all over
its hedge, draws an eye to it long before a nose; although
it can't sense itself touched by human looks, presumably.
But a cat can, as we do – if by now I don't, & happily so.

Lone Star clattering

What got done to me stains
through my hopes of passing

as fully human – though my
'bad blood' won't gloss that;

to canter around its crimson
rosette would tart up a harm

more my post-war bad luck
than a told shame's mother.

Still, the pose: *Say yellow rose
go hard & plain to Amarillo.*

They have shot me down!
Yet do I rise, a tad orange.

'The Sapling'
(after Umberto Saba)

Today is rain. The day's like evening,
the spring's like autumn. Gales ravage
a sapling, well-rooted but not looking it,
lifting above the shrubs – a boy, grown
too tall for his too green age. Pure white
blossom the squall tore off – future fruit,
winter preserves, flowers fallen on grass.
Your vast motherliness grieves for them.

Colour words, person words

Writing one word, *red*, on an empty page will make it start to bleed
          and ooze with scarlet if left unattended.

Pasting the single word *grey* in a blank document can fog up your entire screen.
An isolated *blue* persuades a bare file to look tranquil and composed.

To write the word *she* does less than you might think. Or it does more.
To write the word *she* does more than you might want. Or it does less.
What about *he*? – Well, what about he.
Typing a solitary word, *indifferent*, doesn't do much one way or another.

'You can never get it right, can you.'
– Not as long as you think in two.
You are in twos, poor colourless sexes.

Air

Evening's rose-peach sky
aches in the throat.
Then quizzical dusk –

the fade-out to primrose,
why should it sting?
What is the hurt in that light?

Fishers of men

A bruised sea, barracked by storms.
Now boats go leaping for their shelter.
Salvaging hopes prod fishers of men

towards fresh resurrection grabs —
a human netted, hauled in thrashing,
salt-filmy eyes rocked along a stride

of blurred pines frothed up by grey,
where water slaps the air, where air
drills into water, and seals may lope.

How some things once came

Quant catalogues came sketched on tracing paper.
Tights came as a revelation.
Sobranies came in canary yellow, sky blue, or rosy papers.
Roll-ups usually came undone.
Art postcards came inked in flocks, from friends.
Jam-jar papers came as pearly discs like oyster shell linings.
Abortion Law Reform Association newsletters came in plain wrappers.
Mascara came as oblong cakes in little pans, then came to grief.
Court documents for sole custody of your children came 'served' or thrown at you.
It even came to that.
Forms to prove they'd qualify for free school meals came on blurry lined paper.
People habitually came in twos.
Came apart easily, but so harshly.

Slow burn

Happiness, I consider in my papery season, did zigzag toward me

until later I got hated, in the guise of that demon I was held to be.

Now I forget much, in my white fog pierced by rare if brilliant rays.

My beard careens into spidery threads, long and light on the wind.

Let these scant years keep lucid, unclouded by the familiar sorrows,

and released from their rattle of verdicts, whether issued or received.

Whistling down a meadow path I was frank and easy in my speaking.

My will to trust limped off mutely once it heard honour canter away.

Yet even a single 'But how could they have?' is one plaint too many.

Or do they, like me, pick their consciences to ribbons? Behind my fan

[53]

I could weep for the bruised decades – then, I wouldn't have quivered.

Secretly the intimate talkative skin seals over, turning to face the wall.

A halfhearted recruit to the sect of post-sexuals must quit her soft spot

for 'devotion to something afar' or 'desire of the moth for the star' but

what good to even the keenest-antennae'd of moths could any star be?

I'd bound my own feet in a *luxe* of all-giving, determined to offer them

everything I'd never been given myself. Was that one way of getting it?

The outcome was ivory trotters so polished a blade flips right off them.

Evenings float under television, rather than into amnesiac scholarship

yet my recall of his death threats to me still stays embarrassingly sharp.

As a boy I'd puzzled over what had brought out such cruelty in them –

what was it, I worried, in me. I had never thought of myself as young

so was sheltered by only my plywood shield of bravado. It splintered.

Unknowing, I once had a child 'by' a man who had strangled a swan.

Others grew thin-lipped when the world disappointed them and I was

at hand as its rep. Bad rep. Caustic love-agonists, complacently ageing

wax savvy about therapy. 'Whose are all these children?' the benefits

officer asked me so scathingly it just wasn't on to reply to her: 'Mine'.

Time How Short

What does your wordless absence say.
Who were they for, those promises.
Nothing was true, if now all's gone
though it was – wasn't it – serious.

Hopes denied recoil, then stiffen
like glazed weeds tangled under ice.
Time does not always 'heal the damage'
but tamps it down and seals it tight.

Ears and mouths must close on silence
whose patient night gapes in appeal.
Willed muteness is a short-lived luxury.
Speak as you can & while I still can hear.

Were I September

Late bees grubbing through the trefoil's squeaky-clean yellows

among dock plants blotched with coral or beetroot rust

whose seed-masts toss their ferrous signals to the breeze

as delicate rattles in insect ears, maybe.

Light patter. What authority could my old pain, broadcast, allow me to claim?

– None, I'd say.

The humans sound their billions-fold democracy of distress – a dying spillage.

How clear and plain its songs, how hummable.

Notes

'Committed' reverses Kim Hyesoon's remark: 'Our mothers who have gone are buried in our bodies. It can be said that we were born with dead mothers in our body.' From the interview by Ruth Williams, *Guernica* magazine (online), January 2012.

'Not Olga' is drawn from one of Picasso's portraits of Marie-Thérèse Walter.

'Seaside Rock' first appeared (as 'Lettered Constancy') in *Une Soupe aux Mauvaises Herbes*, a chapbook edited by Joan Scott to mark Elizabeth Weed's 80th birthday, 2020.

'From René Char's vineyard' is made of variations on single lines lifted from a few of Char's poems.

'Lines from Novalis' draws on aphoristic remarks by Georg von Hardenberg [pen-name, 'Novalis'] in his *Notes for a Romantic Encyclopaedia*, 1798, translated by David W. Wood.

'Friend and reader of Horace' is a version of Günter Eich's poem 'Freund und Horazleser'.

'A thing in a room' follows this prompt from W. S. Graham's notebooks: '*To make a poem about some object in this room. To see how it will change the object. (The poem short, 10–14 lines. Maybe better fairly descriptive visually first of all.)*'

'Beggars of Life' is a movie starring Louise Brooks. Among the actors, directors, and cinematographers appearing in this poem are Michelangelo Antonioni, Raoul Coutard, Charles Burnett, Asghar Farhadi, Hirokazu Kore-Eda, Lucrecia Martel, Yasujiro Ozu, Alain Resnais, Jean Vigo and Monica Vitti.

'To a Lady, Viewed By a Head-Louse' reverses the speaker in Robert Burns' 'To a Louse, on Seeing One on a Lady's Bonnet at Church'.

'Another Agony in the Garden' incorporates some details – egrets, rivulets – from Andrea Mantegna's painting of (Christ's) 'Agony in the Garden'.

The figure in section i of 'Three awkward ears' appears in Watteau's painting 'Pierrot' (sometimes titled 'Gilles').

'Songs Without Words' mentions Felix Mendelssohn, who wrote the song cycle with this same title; his motto was (approximately): to compose and to live in a bright and light manner.

'Tick Tock' twists a line by Alexander Pope, 'The sound must seem an echo to the sense', from his poem 'An Essay on Criticism', 1711.

'Plumage House'. This building stands on Shepherdess Walk in Hackney, London. It had once housed the feather merchants H. Bestimt. The last line refers to Virginia Woolf's essay 'The Plumage Bill', on the cruelties of the feather trade, and the question of whose interests sustained it more; the vanity of fashionable hat-buying women, or the commercial greed of businessmen.

The line 'All, as a rule, fall towards their wound' is from Lucretius' *De Rerum Natura*.

'Lurex' includes a line from the traditional Scots ballad and folk song 'O waly, waly'.

'Alice: a fragment' was written to celebrate Alice Notley's 75th birthday in 2020. It mentions her old home on St Mark's Place in New York – as well as some poetry-arguments of the 1970s.

'And as I sit I feel the gaze' takes its title from a line in W. S. Graham's poem 'Mr Le Grice's Portrait Class (A Model's Eye View)':

> *Half-past nine in Truro town*
> *Chimes in the winter-morning air.*
> *Time to begin the portrait class.*
> *The model gazes from his chair.*
> *I gaze out through the twisting glass*
> *That twists a seagull as it flies*
> *And as I sit I feel the gaze*
> *Of all the portrait painting eyes.*

'The Sapling, after Saba' is a shortened version of Umberto Saba's 'L'arboscello' from his 1910 collection *Casa e Campagna* in *Songbook; The Selected Poems of Umberto Saba*, translated by G. Hochfield and L. Nathan.

'Time How Short' was written as a 'guest' inclusion for Agnes Lehòczky's *Pool Epitaphs* (2017) and again in her *Swimming Pool* (2017).

Acknowledgements

My heartfelt thanks, once more, to Don Paterson.

I'm very grateful to the editors of the online or paper publications in which some of the poems first appeared:

Die Deeper Into Life (2017), *Tender* (2017), *Blackbox Manifold* (2017), *Times Literary Supplement* (2018, 2019), *London Review of Books* (2018, 2021), *Try To Be Better* (2019), *Chicago Review*, USA (2018), *According to John James* (2018), *Golden Handcuffs Review*, USA (2019), *The Caught Habits of Language* (2018), *Poetry Review* (2017, 2019), *Poetry*, USA (2017), *Pool* (2017), *Swimming Pool* (2018), *Cumulus* (2018), *Face Press* (2018), *Poetry London* vol.9 (2019), *Guardian Saturday Review* (27/04/2019), *Une Soupe aux Mauvaises Herbes*, USA (2020), *Poetry Ireland Review* vol.132 (2020).